GOOD MORNING, LORD

Devotions for Campers

Floyd and Pauline Todd

BAKER BOOK HOUSE
Grand Rapids, Michigan

TO
Dellno Marshall Higbee
and
Bessie Turnidge Higbee
parents, pastors, teachers, camp leaders
whose lives have influenced
countless persons Christward

PREFACE

Is there a place for a book of devotions for campers?

Yes! Consider these possible locations:

. . . in the glove compartment of the family car, wedged between road maps, a smashed box of Kleenex, and a can of mosquito repellent.

. . . in the side pocket of a guitar case, crammed in with the latest Christian folk music, property of a turned-on-to-Christ young camper.

. . . on the bedside stand of a golden-ager in a tidy camp cottage, neatly stacked beside a worn Bible.

. . . in the suitcase under the creaky bed of the young counselor, sandwiched between yesterday's socks and tomorrow's tee shirt.

. . . in the miniature cabinet of an aluminum-sided camper, lurching back and forth as the retired couple's pickup starts and stops.

Today's increasing number of campers are bound together in a common bond: to "get away from it all" and to find healing of spirits in the out-of-doors.

This "getting away" involves leaving behind familiar religious patterns. How easy it is for Christians on private camping trips to forget family devotions or private moments alone with Christ. Even at Christian camps, the schedule may be so full that communion time with Christ is neglected.

As we prepared this volume, the following persons and their needs were particularly kept in mind:

. . . families, couples, singles on private camping trips. To help them maintain family worship or individual devotional times.

. . . counselors at youth camps. To provide materials for their cabin devotional periods or times of informal outdoor worship.

. . . campers in organized camps, from young teens to young nineties. To offer materials for devotions in keeping with the outdoor setting.

The overall objective of this volume is to help all campers (vacationers of all stripes are invited to rally round) to draw closer to Christ and to be more aware of His marvels in nature. What lessons He teaches as creator!

Floyd and Pauline Todd

Warm Beach, Washington
September 1972

1. TRAIL MARKERS

The Lord shall guide thee continually. —
Isaiah 58:11

Trapper Ronald Woodcock had been lost for thirty days in the wilderness of Upper British Columbia. Tortuously he had fought his way through underbrush, following the banks of streams, hoping to find civilization. Suddenly he spied a rotting telegraph pole. "If I can only follow this old government trail, I'll make it!" For twenty-seven more days he searched for the packed earth of the trail, for bits of wire and old poles. Exhausted, clothes tattered, sick from an all-berry diet, flesh perforated with mosquito bites, he stumbled onto a dirt road, to passing motorists, help, and home.

Indians and early trappers were expert in marking trails. A tied clump of grass, a blazed tree, or a stack of rocks meant "You're on the trail." A bent clump of grass, a bent bush, or arrows on the ground made of sticks or stones meant "Turn this way."

God has not left His children to stumble through the maze of life with no trail markers. What joy it is in following the Christian way to suddenly recognize that God has sent clear guidance. Our heavenly Father may use a Scripture verse or a word from one of His servants. But the Christian recognizes it. To him it says, "This is God's way of guiding me right now. He's going to help me through this wilderness."

My Lord knows the way through the wilderness;
All I have to do is follow.

2. CEDAR TREE

*I will delight myself in thy statutes: I will not
forget thy word.*—Psalm 119:6

"Cedar tree! Cedar tree!" chanted the young campers
as they spied yet another conifer along the forest trail.
At hike's beginning the counselor had urged, "Watch
for the cedar foliage: flat and branched, chartreuse new
growth, unforgettable aroma. For the Indians who once
lived here, the cedar tree was the essential of life."

Puget Sound Indians found the straight grain of the
red cedar (*Thuja plicata*) easy to split without axe or
saw. Its resin protected it from rot and insects; its light-
ness made it easy to carve and carry. Canoes in which
warriors ventured into the Pacific were cedar logs hol-
lowed by controlled burning. Baskets were woven of its
splints; pounded strands of bark were woven into skirts
and mats or supplied tinder for starting fires without
matches. Communal houses—often two hundred feet long
—were sided with treasured, wide planks, attached to
crosspieces with thongs. Tribal artists carved meaningful totem poles of cedar. The cultural pattern of these
Indians centered in this tree.

The pattern of life for democratic nations centers in
the Biblical belief of the worth of the individual and the
brotherhood of man. Without the Bible, as in commu-
nism, the state is supreme; the individual is expendable.

The whole life of the Christian centers in God's Word.
It guides, protects, warms, inspires, and gives light along
the way.

3. GIFT GIVERS

Freely ye have received, freely give.—Matthew 10:8

The Lummi, Haida, Snohomish, and other Northwest Indian tribes had it made! Early residents of the Puget Sound-British Columbia shores are said to have been the best-fed, best-housed, best-clothed Indians in America.

They lived where clams, crabs, oysters, ducks, and geese abounded. Deer roamed the forests. Salmon in multitudes spawned in the rivers. Summertime brought ripening of over twenty-five varieties of berries. Dried and rolled into balls, they were a year-round Indian delicacy. Cedar houses were expertly engineered. One longhouse is said to have housed one thousand Indians at the mouth of the Snohomish River. Deerskin, cedar bark, and reeds from the tideflats were used in making clothing, bedding, and storage facilities. All this bounty God gave freely.

These Indians were also givers. The *potlatch* was a time of feasting, singing, dancing, and games. Then the host gave gifts, leaving himself a poor man. But not for long. He knew that all who received a gift from him—a canoe, cedar plank, basket, dog, or shell—must return a gift of greater value. Actually he had invested his money at a good rate of interest.

Motives in giving—how they differ! God freely gave His Son for undeserving, sinful man. Man's response must also be selfless. Not: "I'll give my life to You, Lord; but I expect it back with interest." Nor: I'll do this for You, Lord, if You'll do that." But a free gift: "No matter what life brings, my life is Yours."

> My life, my all I give to Thee,
> O Thou, who died on Calvary.

4. COMING APART

Come you yourselves apart into a desert place and rest awhile.—Mark 6:31

"That rocker may collapse if one more person sits in it," worried Mrs. Robbins. Tired ones had rocked and rested in it on the front porch for years. But now it was definitely coming apart. Alternating humid and hot weather had loosened the glued rounds. Mrs. Robbins decided, "I'll send it to Jim's repair shop; and while I'm at it, I'll have it refinished." When the renovated rocker was returned, Mrs. Robbins gloated, "That old wood is beautiful. From now on this goes in my living room!"

Under the stress of modern life too many persons are "coming apart." Some are in varying stages of disintegration: morally, emotionally, spiritually.

One may be the teen-ager, tempted by his peers: "Get with it, man! Everyone's doing it!"

Or the tired young mother who exclaims, "Where do these youngsters get all this energy?"

Or the man tense from the unremitting demands of making it in a competitive world who thunders, "How much more of this can I stand?"

Or the mature person carrying life's burdens who sighs, "One more trouble and I may collapse."

To those who feel so pressured, Christ says again, as He did long ago to His harried disciples, "Come ye apart!" Camp may be the place where the Master Repairman ministers in healing of spirits. A few days of "coming apart" with Jesus may offer a cure for "coming apart" at the seams. A whole new life of usefulness may lie ahead.

5. POLLUTION CLEANSED

*Wash me thoroughly from mine iniquity, and
cleanse me from my sin.*—Psalm 51:2

Onward ever, lovely river, softly calling to the sea,
Time that scars us, maims and mars us
Leaves no track nor trace on thee.

Joaquin Miller penned these lines about the "Beautiful Willamette" when ecology was a word known only to scientists. "From the Cascades' frozen gorges, leaping like a child at play," this river wends its way through one of the world's loveliest and most fruitful valleys. At Portland, the river slips between its guardian snow-capped ranges to merge with the mighty Columbia.

Poet Miller did not foresee the effect increased population and industry would have on the Willamette. Pollution rose as raw sewage from valley towns and effluents from six hundred industries poured into the river. "Maimed and marred," it was one of the filthiest rivers in the nation.

But conservationists battled. "Clean up the Willamette" became a political issue. Tough laws were passed and enforced. In only a few years salmon again fought their way upstream to spawn. Swimmers and boaters again enjoyed their tree-lined river. Highest federal standards of purity were met. Continued vigilance is keeping the Willamette clean.

Carelessness, contamination, concern, cleansing, continued vigilance is the sequence in the rebirth of a river. Is it so different from spiritual rebirth? God's never-changing laws of purity set the standard.

6. HIDDEN RICHES

*And I will give thee the treasures of darkness,
and hidden riches of secret places.*—Isaiah
45:3

"Hound dog, what are you finding in that gopher
hole?" asked young Bradford, who had gone to the woods
with his brother to shoot meat for supper. At the turn of
the century the Bradfords lived in the typical poor man's
house: a frame, unpainted shack with porch across the
front, set in the hills of southern Indiana. Their forest
land was too hilly for much successful farming. It lay
in the "terminal moraines" (southernmost deposits) of
the great glaciers which once had covered mid-America.

As the brothers watched, the hound's back feet began
spraying out a fine-textured sand. Experts later declared
the sand perfect for use in foundry castings. The hound
had uncovered a fortune.

In a few years the brothers left their shack, building
an imposing manor house on the brow of the hill over-
looking the White River valley. After a long life the
bachelor brothers willed their land for the benefit of
the children of Indiana. Today several children's camps
are sheltered in its hardwood forests. Headquarters of
the American Camping Association are there. Indiana
University uses the manor house as a facility in its outdoor education program. Many lives have been enriched
by Bradford generosity.

How many persons live in spiritual poverty while so
near at hand, with a little digging, are the undiscovered
bounties of God's resources? How many seemingly com-
monplace persons, discovering God's plan for them, go
forth to bless the world? God is still in the business of
making the poor rich in spiritual treasure.

7. REST STOP AHEAD

Hope in God, for I shall yet praise him.—
Psalm 43:5

Chicago's clotted traffic lay miles behind. Straight down the South Dakota highway the family Chevrolet pointed its dusty nose. Mile after mile the road stretched on limitlessly. Flat farmland and grazing land gave a feeling of space enough and to spare. But the children complained, "Isn't this ever going to end?" Then came Rapid City and the delightful beauty of the Black Hills. Tree-covered hillsides and mountain streams were the more refreshing after the sameness of the prairie.

A nonair-conditioned Rambler took the family across California's Mohave Desert. The blazing sun highlighted the stark beauty of the rocky, mountainous landscape. No shade, not even one tree, offered respite for the over-heated travelers. "What's that ahead?" asked a youngster. "A service station, plus one tree," answered dad. "We'll stop there!" As the children tumbled out of the car, they made for the tree. Said brother Frank, "Compared to some trees, it's really not so great; but its shade really feels good here!"

How like traveling is life. Sometimes the way is monoto-nous, barren, rough, difficult. Then one's prayer may be: "Help me, God, to see the beauty and meaning in this desert experience." But just as surely as hard places come, they will end; and life will have its refreshing moments. Then one's prayer may be : "Thank You, God, for the hard places that helped me better to appreciate this beauty. Keep me as close to You now as when my need seemed greater."

8. WILD FOOD

I will feed my flock . . . saith the Lord God.
—Ezekiel 34:15

Euell Gibbons of Maine teaches solo survival to young people. They learn to find, prepare, and (sometimes) even enjoy nutritious wild food. At completion of the course each student is marooned on an uninhabited island with no food except what he can forage. None have starved. Yet many untrained wanderers starve with much edible food nearby.

Ground nuts helped the Pilgrims survive that first desperate winter. Forty-niners warded off scurvy by eating miner's lettuce. Pioneers unknowingly obtained vitamin C in teas brewed from leaves of fireweed, bayberry, clover, strawberries, and rose hips. Wild greens of plantain, nettles, pigweed, purslane, and marsh marigolds were relished by Indians and by today's wild food enthusiasts. Berries and nuts are easily-gathered wild delicacies.

Many times God takes His people off their familiar diet of church on Sunday and weekly prayer meetings. Many servicemen as well as travelers know the feeling, "What will sustain me spiritually now?"

But God will feed His flock wherever He leads them. In new circumstances it may take unusual effort to find spiritual food. The foodstuff may be as different, yet as vaguely similar, as the taste of the cattail's tender stalks is to cucumbers. But the seeking Christian will survive!

9. WEED SEEDS

The Lord knows how to deliver the godly out of temptation.—II Peter 2:9

Cockleburs on his socks and grass seed in his shoes will make any hiker aware of the millions of maturing seeds. A single stalk of rye grass may bear half a million. In spite of the tons of seeds devoured by birds, plus those that fall into the water to rot, enough survive to assure us of plenty of weeds another season. Some stay alive in the soil, not to sprout for years.

As Keith approached, his neighbor Inga straightened from her weeding. "I've come for the rhubarb roots you offered," he explained. "How long have you had this garden on the hilltop?"

She was slight but sturdy in spite of her years. Inga smiled, "I'm seventy-three. My parents came over from Norway before I was born and settled here. This has always been the garden."

"And you still have weeds?"

Chuckling, Inga walked to the garden's edge to pluck a fluffy dandelion head. "Count the seeds. Do you think there are enough to replace that one plant next spring? Birds and wind bring them to our soil. Gardeners fight weeds forever."

Christians fight temptations forever. Satan's supply never runs low. "I've had new temptations since I moved here," sobbed one Christian seeking new strength in Christ. Satan does vary his attacks with changing circumstances: peer pressures for the young, family and job tensions for the middle years, self-pity and loneliness for the aging. But greater than the tempter is God! He will deliver those who call on Him.

10. PRAISE FESTIVAL

Praise ye the Lord. Praise God in his sanctuary.—Psalm 150:1

When was Jesus a camper? Every year from the time He was twelve, He was required by Hebrew law to camp out for seven days. He and His father went annually to the Feast of Tabernacles at Jerusalem. Held just after the harvest, this was a time of praise to God.

Can you imagine Jesus as a young teen arriving in Jerusalem, greeting friends He had not seen since the last festival? No doubt He helped Joseph build their bower of tree branches. These tree tents reminded the people of the days of wandering in the wilderness. Dotting the temple area and the flat rooftops, spilling outside the city walls, the bowers offered places for quiet communion and personal thanksgiving.

But all was not quietness. In the temple thousands watched Levites lead impressive rituals and sacred concerts by massed choirs. What great memories Jesus carried home: the joy of personal communion with God in the bower, the high moments of praise in the crowded temple, the times of fellowship with friends.

As they camp today, Christians can be similarly thankful. They can sense that wherever God is praised, that site becomes His sanctuary.

11. SIGHT UNSEEN

He knoweth the way I take.—Job 23:10

Mountain winds temper the summer sun at Paradise Lodge. Breathtakingly close, snow-crowned Mount Rainier rears its regal crest. Cars, campers, and trailers from across the continent wait in the parking lot, still curbed with winter snow. Around the lodge, haunted by skiers all winter, tourists seem intoxicated with the overwhelming beauty about them. Standing at the guard rail, some gaze at jewellike Paradise Valley stretching away at their feet, a mile above sea level.

This tiny alpine meadow has so recently aroused from its winter blanket of snow. Now a patchwork of riotously colored wildflowers covers it. Indian paintbrush, wild lupine, and a score of their floral cousins are in their moment of glory. Yet in this high country there are uncounted wild flowers in similar alpine meadows that will bloom, seed, and die, never seen by human eyes.

The poet Thomas Gray observed: "Full many a flower is born to blush unseen, and waste its sweetness on the desert air." Many a heroic deed, many a kindness, many an exemplary life will send forth its sweetness seemingly unnoticed—with no headlines, no marble monument, no presidential citation.

High on the scaffold in the Basilica of Saint Peter's in Rome, Michelangelo painted his frescoed masterpiece. In an obscure corner where it would never be seen, the artist worked carefully. His assistant asked, "Why do you take such pains there, where no one will know?" "I will know," answered the artist. And God will know!

12. BEAUTY MAKER

Now to him who is able to keep you from falling and to present you without blemish before the presence of his glory. . . .—Jude 24.

Albert Schweitzer ranks among the great missionary heroes. Yet as a child, he was a slow scholar. Besides, he had unruly hair. A peasant girl, working in his parents' German parsonage, once scolded, "Hair shows a person's character. Yours is the worst I've seen!" Young Albert was discouraged, until one day while visiting his grandmother he saw a great artist's picture of the Apostle John—with unruly hair! Albert mused, "He is a real saint. I can't be all bad; God can use me, too."

By the time he was thirty, Albert was a concert pianist, author, and college president. But he gave these up to study medicine and then "bury himself" in French Equatorial Africa. For the rest of his long life, God made Albert's life a thing of beauty and blessing in the famous Lambaréné hospital.

> God, who touchest earth with beauty
> Make me lovely, too,
> With Thy Spirit recreate me,
> Make my heart anew.
> Like Thy springs and running waters
> Make me crystal pure,
> Like Thy rocks of towering grandeur
> Make me strong and sure.
> Like the arching of the heavens,
> Lift my thoughts above;
> Turn my dreams to noble action,
> Ministries of love.
>
> —Mary S. Edgar

13. EAGLE'S WINGS

But they that wait upon the Lord . . . shall mount up with wings as eagles.—Isaiah 40:31

"Find the eagles' nest!" Year after year this was the assignment for new campers at a Wyoming camp. Returning campers kept their own knowledge secret. Binoculars focused skyward whenever the eagle pair soared above the camp. Before camp was over, most campers had spotted the nest in a cleft high on the cliff above the camp. There the eagle pair raised their eaglets in a six-foot nest of interlaced branches.

Found across America, the majestic bald eagle deserves to be the national bird. Nearly three feet long, its wingspread may be over seven feet. Its distinctive white head —feathered, not bald—accounts for its name. Now eagles have become "an endangered species," slated for extinction unless man changes his ways.

Anyone who has watched an eagle raise his wings horizontal to his body and take off for the heavens cannot but be inspired. Higher and higher the eagle soars until he becomes a dot in the blue canopy of sky.

As one considers the eagle, Isaiah's words become so meaningful. Waiting on God does give renewal of strength. Prayer gives wings to mount to heaven's door, perseverance to keep on running the race of life, and courage to walk on in the Christian way.

14. SUN OF MY SOUL

*The Sun of righteousness shall arise with heal-
ing in his wings.*—Malachi 4:2

The sun dominates the life and thinking of the Japanese. Nippon, the word for their country, means "base
of the sun." According to tradition their emperor is a
direct descendant of the sun, hence, a god. The Japanese
flag features the red, rising sun. Houses are all built to
face the southeast, with windows in front for viewing the
rising sun. Pious Buddhists arise before sunup to greet
the first rays with prayer and ritual.

The sun is earth's nearest star, ninety-three million
miles away. All nine planets and their thirty-one moons
revolve around it. It bombards the earth with energy from
its nuclear furnace where hydrogen is changed to helium.
The sun causes all earth's weather. Solar heat strikes the
varying surfaces of the earth. Air thus heated in varying
degrees creates air currents, generating winds and storms.
Without the sun there could be no plant, animal, or human life.

No wonder that from the beginning of time men have
worshiped the sun. But the Christian worships the God
who made the sun. To the Christian, God is the answer
to all of life—as essential as the sun to earth life.

> Sun of my soul, Thou Saviour dear,
> It is not night if Thou art near;
> O may no earthborn cloud arise,
> To shut me from my Saviour's eyes.
> Abide with me from morn to eve,
> For without Thee I cannot live.

15. WHO WAS HERE?

For none of us liveth to himself, and no man dieth to himself.—Romans 14:7

"Kilroy was here!" A war-weary public scratched this World War II graffito in almost any public place. "Who's Kilroy?" No one really cared. Some explained that he was an individual who signed inspection sheets with these soon-to-be-famous three words. The signs multiplied. America, relieving its war tensions, chuckled at this nonsense.

"Raccoon was here!" say the two inward turned, five-toed tracks followed by two smaller ones that look like midget, baby handprints. The doe's dainty hooves leave evidence that she stopped by the mud of the creek bank to drink. The domestic cat leaves his identifying marks on the lawn's new-fallen snow. Today making plaster casts of animal tracks is an enjoyable camp craft.

But without graffiti, mud or plaster casts, or new-fallen snow, every person leaves an influence that says, "I was here!" Every camp is better or worse in some degree because of the action and words of each camper. Longfellow expresses this truth:

> Lives of great men all remind us
> We can make our lives sublime,
> And departing, leave behind us
> Footprints on the sands of time.
> Footprints, that perhaps another
> Sailing o'er life's solemn main,
> A forlorn and shipwrecked brother
> Seeing, shall take heart again.

16. MORNING PRAISE

This is the day which the Lord hath made; we will rejoice and be glad in it.—Psalm 118:24

Still, still with Thee, when purple morning breaketh,
When the birds wake and the shadows flee,
Dearer than morning, lovelier than daylight
Dawns the sweet consciousness, I am with Thee.

Millet's masterpiece, *Song of the Lark,* depicts a peasant girl already at work in the fields, though the sun has just pushed over the horizon. Muted colors do not diminish the power of the picture. The maiden's posture and expression make the viewer thrill with her and almost hear the tiny lark trill his morning praise.

A minister recounts, "In order to make my next appointment in another state, I had risen before dawn to drive the ruler-straight roads of western Texas. Suddenly a gold-orbed sun burst over the eastern sky. Glorious pinks and purples reflected across the heavens, brushstrokes of the Master Artist. Mornings from that time have been special for me. It may be foggy where I am, but I know that the golden sun is there with its promise of another day with Christ."

Since God made the day, the sunrise, and each of His children, why not rejoice in the morning?

When morning gilds the skies,
My heart awakening cries:
May Jesus Christ be praised.

17. GUITAR AND DRUM

*For in him we live and move and have our
being.*—Acts 17:28

Guitars lent their harmony to the haunting melody of
the song. Drums rhythmically added emphasis. Young
men and women in current dress and hair styles draped
informally around the campfire. But only the wood smoke
drifted heavenward—no "pot," no tobacco. For this was
a church youth group at a weekend retreat. Young faces
glowed as they sang:

> In the stars His handiwork I see,
> On the wind He speaks with majesty,
> Though He ruleth over land and sea,
> What is that to me?
> I will celebrate Nativity,
> For it has a place in history,
> Sure, He came to set His people free,
> What is that to me?

Then Mark interrupted. "Man, that's just like it was for
me! Sure, I looked at the sky and agreed more or less that
God must have made the stars. I knew about the Jews, and
I celebrated nativity—Christmas. But what was that to
me? Nothing! But nothing! Then something happened
really great. I met Jesus! Really met Him face to face."
As Mark sang on triumphantly, others hummed:

> Now He walks beside me day by day,
> Ever watching o'er me lest I stray,
> Helping me to find that narrow way,
> HE'S EVERYTHING TO ME![1]

A face-to-face encounter with Christ instantly changes
head religion to heart-felt religion.

18. SMALL IMPORTANCE

*God hath chosen the weak things of the world
to confound the things which are mighty.*—
I Corinthians 1:27

"Ladybug, ladybug, fly away home!" Who has not
warned a ladybug to rescue her children from the flames?
Probably few of these persons know or care that there
are 4,300 known species of ladybugs, 370 in America.
But everyone likes the little red beetle with the polka dot
jacket, especially farmers.

Some years ago the cottony cushion scale from Aus-
tralia was accidentally introduced into California, killing
thousands of citrus trees. Then a species of ladybugs, *Ro-
dalis cardinals,* was imported. Their appetite for scale
bugs saved an industry worth a hundred million dollars
today. Now entomologists are studying these "living pes-
ticides," hoping to reduce the need for chemicals.

One can cram 70,000 ladybugs into a gallon container.
They are small, but to the alfalfa farmers of California's
Central Valley they are essential. One farmer's field may
harbor half a million hungry ladybug larvae, feasting on
aphids that would ruin the crop.

Many of God's children are not great in the eyes of
man; but to God, they are important as they faithfully
cooperate in the work He assigns.

Hide not thy talent in the earth, however small it be,
Its faithful use, its utmost worth
God will require of thee. . . .
The humblest service rendered here He will as truly own
As Paul's in his exalted sphere
Or Gabriel's near the throne.
Go then and strive to do thy part though humble it may
  be;
The ready hand and willing heart
Are all heaven asks of thee.

—William Cutler

19. GOOD FISHING

I will make you fishers of men.—Mark 1:17

The tree-lined river in North Dakota flowed swiftly by the dock. There campers were baiting hooks and casting lines. "There are good fish holes here," Eric told his friend. The camp cook had agreed to a late evening fish fry if the boys caught enough fish. By sundown enough perch and catfish had been landed for a great fish feed after evening vespers.

Christ one day asked His disciples, "Boys, have you caught any fish?" Then He gave them a lesson in fishing. Another time He promised that they would become "fishers of men."

The good fisherman finds pleasure in fishing, uses the right bait, has correct tackle, goes where the fish are, and skillfully uses his equipment.

The successful soul winner has joy in leading others to Christ, knows that Christ's love and forgiveness are the bait, and that his own friendliness and Christ-likeness are the tackle. He must fish for souls where they are, with the power and skill of a Spirit-directed life.

A famous lawyer nearing death once said, "I wish I had gone fishing more."

Today is the day God has given for the Christian to avoid future regrets about lost opportunities in soul winning.

> Lead me to some soul today,
> Oh, teach me, Lord, just what to say.

20. CONTACT

Call upon me and I will answer thee.—Jeremiah 33:3

Fresh from the bush and his African kraal, the Zulu tribesman visited the city for the first time. He was fascinated as he watched a man in a telephone booth. The man talked, laughed, and gestured with his hands. The Zulu circled the booth, then finally left, shaking his head, "A crazy man in a cage talking to a box," he judged. What the Zulu did not know was that there was a connection working according to scientific principles that enabled friends to communicate.

The unbeliever may ridicule the Christian as he prays, "You are only talking to yourself!" What the atheist does not understand is that there is a connection between man and God working according to spiritual laws.

If radio's slim fingers can catch a melody
From night, and toss it over a continent or sea,
If the petaled white notes of a violin
Are blown across a mountain or a city's din,
If songs, like crimson roses
Are culled from the thin blue air—
Why should mortals wonder if God answers prayer?
—Ethel Romig Fuller

God answers prayer in the morning;
God answers prayer at noon;
God answers prayer in the evening;
So keep your heart in tune.

Frank Laubach wrote, "Prayer at its highest is a two-way conversation; and for me, the most important part is listening for God's replies."

21. PRAYING HANDS

I thank thee, and praise thee, O thou God of my fathers.—Daniel 2:23

Wheeling along the interstate highway in Louisiana, the family was on the way home from a camping trip. After pointed suggestions from his teen-agers, Dad pulled off to a hamburger stand.

Freda pointed to an insect on the outside of the stand. "Wow, what a big grasshopper!"

"That's no grasshopper," Bruce corrected. "That's a praying mantis. We've studied them in biology. When they feed, they hold up their hands—I guess they are really forelegs—as if they are praying."

"Better than some people," commented Freda.

In one of his most popular paintings, Norman Rockwell, beloved folk painter of America, depicts a crowded small restaurant. In a booth grandma and small grandson clasp their hands in prayer to thank God before eating. Those nearby watch with nostalgic expressions. Are they remembering their own early training?

An editor commented on this picture, "As long as one generation teaches another gratitude to God for daily blessings, too much can't be wrong with America."

Daily blessings—how easy it is to forget to thank God for them! Simply but forcefully, this mealtime prayer used in camps expresses gratitude:

> We thank Thee for the morning light,
> For rest and shelter of the night,
> For health and food, for love and friends,
> For everything Thy goodness sends. Amen.

22. BUSINESS WITH GOD

As the Lord hath called everyone, so let him walk.—I Corinthians 7:17

Senora Esther Harris Decoud fills a large place in Paraguay. American born, she is the wife of Dr. Reinaldo Decoud, leading Protestant scholar, medical doctor, university professor. Dr. Decoud, fluent in several languages, set himself to translating the entire Bible into the vernacular of the Paraguayan Indians. Esther tells of her call to missionary work which led her to Paraguay and to marriage with this Christian leader.

"I had graduated from a Christian college and taught school awhile. Even though I was active in the church, it was with reluctance that I agreed to help at children's camp. I did not realize what God was planning for me there. In the camp's splendid spiritual atmosphere, I got down to business with God about my future. Alone in the woods, I made my consecration to offer myself as a missionary."

Getting down to business with God can occur at camp or elsewhere. The important part is to respond whenever or wherever He calls.

> I heard Him call,
> "Come follow," that was all.
> My gold grew dim;
> My soul went after Him.
> I rose and followed,
> That was all.
> Who would not follow
> If he heard Him call?

23. GOD'S FOOTPRINTS

Thou canst not see my face, for there shall no man see me and live.—Exodus 33:20

Thus did God deny Moses' request. But Moses was not the last to seek a face-to-face revelation of God.

On a hilltop above the camp, Patty felt close to God as she lay in the warm sunshine watching clouds drift by. "Please, God, let me see your face." But the clouds kept drifting, the sun kept shining, no face of God appeared.

But God does have ways of revealing Himself to man. God is clearly revealed in His Word, the Bible. Then God sent His Son, Jesus, to reveal God in human form. Another way God reveals Himself is through His creation. Nature reveals God.

God's versatility as a creator is witnessed by the beauty of the sunrise and sunset, in the variety of plants and flowers, in the wonders of animal life: insects, birds, small creatures. Only an all-intelligent God could have planned the harmony of the heavens, the plant-animal food cycle, the rain-river-ocean-cloud water cycle. All about is the signature of God in nature.

An Englishman, traveling in Egypt, thought himself to be an atheist. He hired as a guide a Coptic Christian youth. As they camped in the desert at night, the Englishman teased: "How do you know there is a God? Have you ever seen Him?" "No," replied the youth, "but I know that a camel goes by because I see his footprints. That setting sun on the mountains to me is the footprint of God."

24. SACRIFICE FOR YOUR DELIGHT

The Son of man came . . . to give his life a ransom for many.—Matthew 20:28

The glow of firelight reflected in earnest faces. On this last night of camp many were expressing their joy in Christ and their determination to be steadfast Christians.

Hubert stood, a small book in his hand. "I just discovered the poet John Oxenham at this camp. He's okay. When he looked at a campfire, he saw sacrifice: wood giving its life to give us light and heat. Christ gave His life, too, to bring us salvation. In the same way I want to give my life for Christ and others."

> Kneel always when you light a fire!
> Kneel reverently, and thankful be
> For God's unfailing charity,
> And on the ascending flame inspire
> A little prayer, that shall upbear
> The incense of your thankfulness
> For this sweet grace of warmth and light!
> For here again is sacrifice for your delight.
> Within the wood that lived a joyous life
> Through sunny days and rainy days
> And winter storms and strife; . . .
> God enshrined his sunshine and enwombed
> For you these stores of light and heat
> Your life-joys to complete.
> These all have died that you might live; . . .
> Kneel always when you light a fire,
> Kneel reverently and grateful be
> For God's unfailing charity!

Used by permission of Miss Theodora Dunkerley, Sussex, England.

25. RENEWAL

Thou renewest the face of the earth.—Psalm
104:20

The ecology-minded camper was outraged. "That bull-
dozer has ruined this gorgeous trail!" she sputtered. "Wait
till I see that camp manager!" He calmed her, "Be patient.
Have faith in God's ability to renew His earth."

Another summer the camper returned to check her
favorite trail. Wider now, the trail again was a thing of
beauty. Lacy-leafed trees held hands above hikers. Lush
fern and greenery of bush and grasses covered the scarred
earth.

Poet and novelist Helen Hunt Jackson of California
suffered a double tragedy. Her husband was accidentally
killed; a week later she lost her only child. Feeling her
life scarred beyond help, she secluded herself. After her
bleak winter of mourning, she emerged calm and with a
new purpose: to help the neglected Indians of her area.
Her book *Ramona* is said to have done as much for the
Indians as *Uncle Tom's Cabin* did earlier for black people.

Tragedy or disruption is inevitable in life's journey.
Frustration and doubt are the natural, instinctive reac-
tions. But the Christian must have faith in a God who
prunes with purpose.

> God is a zealous pruner,
> For He knows—
> Who, falsely tender, spares the knife
> But spoils the rose.

26. CAMPING MAGIC

Bless the Lord, O my soul, and forget not all his benefits.—Psalm 103:2

Many have been inspired by the following beautiful passage, printed and reprinted in camping literature.

"Where lies the magic of camping? Truly there is no single answer. It can be different things to different campers. But it weaves a strong spell. It is the little things, half remembered but never wholly forgotten, that come flooding back in future years at the glint of sunlight on still water, the scent of pine forest or woodsmoke, the endless, eternal canopy of night stars. It is the undying heritage of childhood that never fully leaves an adult. . . .

"It is part of the American heritage, from the days when buffalo ran wild and our Red Brothers were masters of woods and streams. Deep in the heart of every child lies the precious spirit of adventure, and it is the warmth of this spirit that grows with camping.

"Who can measure the silence of the deep woods, the peace of the out-of-doors, the spirit of brotherhood that dwells in such surroundings? Can one hope to recapture that priceless moment, when, sleeping under countless stars, one feels the nearness to Things Eternal and catches a fleeting glimpse of the true power and majesty of God?"[1]

---

[1]Charles R. Jenkins, *Light from a Thousand Campfires,* ed., Kenneth Webb (New York: Association Press, 1960), pp. 365-66.

27. BIG BILL

*If any man offend not in words, the same is
a perfect man.*—James 3:2

"A little down on a big bill!" Some clever advertis-
ing man dreamed up this slogan for his furniture store
client. The billboard showed a pelican with a bit of
downy feather on his storage-bin bill. This strutting bird
must have helped sell warehouses of furniture.

Birds' bills are perfectly adapted to their diet require-
ments. The crane's rapier slashes sharply into the water
for fish. Hawk and eagle flesh-eaters easily tear their prey
with their hooked bills. The hummingbird's stiletto delves
for nectar into the long spurs of flowers. Sturdy beaks
enable grouse to scratch for a living, while the wood-
pecker's drill provides him with bugs from bark.

One sometimes hears, "What kind of bird is he, any-
way?" as an inquiry about a person. Like birds, mouths
of humans may identify them. In meeting new persons
while camping or traveling, one listens, then naturally
evaluates. Are they polite, discourteous, quarrelsome,
peaceful, jolly, or sour? Their mouths give them away.

Scripture gives counsel about controlling one's tongue.
But the heart is the culprit. If it is full of resentment or
ill will, there will be evil speaking. Only a heart kept full
of God's love will keep the tongue in control.

> Lord, fill my mouth with worthwhile stuff
> And nudge me when I've said enough.

28. POWER

But ye shall receive power after that the Holy Ghost is come upon you: and ye shall be witnesses. . . .—Acts 1:8

Shirley was an extrovert, game for anything. From a nearby camp, her cabin group and counselor were on a field trip to the American Museum of Atomic Power at Oak Ridge, Tennessee. When the tour guide asked for a volunteer for a trick demonstration, Shirley offered, "I'll do it!" As power was turned on to flow harmlessly through her body, she wondered why the crowd laughed. She was unaware that her hair was standing straight from her head like porcupine quills.

Atomic power burst on the world's consciousness with the devastation of Nagasaki and Hiroshima. But Oak Ridge is dedicated to utilization of this power in peaceful means, more serious than the trick effect on Shirley.

Jesus spoke of power. His promise of the Holy Spirit to His disciples was the promise of power to witness wherever they were.

Billy Graham states: "Men who have moved the world have been Spirit-filled. Filled with the Spirit, the first disciples turned the world upside down. . . . The tides of civilization have risen, the courses of nations have been changed and the pages of history have been brightened by men who have been filled with the Spirit of God."

> Spirit of the Living God, fall afresh on me,
> Melt me, mold me, fill me, use me.

29. VALUING PRAYER

Tell God every detail of your need in earnest and thankful prayer.—Philippians 4:6, (Phillips)

Bill Gillam lifted his melodious voice in praise to God. His words were Spanish. His concert hall was a shack on a tree-lined river in Colombia.

Later his friend B. H. Pearson remonstrated, "Bill, you poured out your songs as though you were singing to thousands."

Bill answered, "I have only one way to sing." He had only one way to live, whether in Colombia, in Haiti, or in America. His gift of music was equaled only by the radiance of his Spirit-directed life. But a brain tumor held him helpless. In the hospital bed he was unable to move or feed himself. Yet his single purpose remained: to witness for Christ. He murmured, "I love you, I love the doctors, I love those who care for me, I love everyone." He left this life radiating Christ's love.

Like all Christians who feel the shortening of life's cord, he had searched his heart. "I would pray more if I had my life to live over again," he confessed. If great Christian Bill Gillam felt this way, should not each Christian examine himself, "Am I valuing prayer sufficiently?"

Prayer is the asking for guidance divine,
Prayer is the clasping of God's hand in mine,
Prayer is the striving to do the Lord's will,
Prayer is the listening to God's voice so still,
Prayer is the asking that others may be
Brought into fellowship, Father, with Thee;
Prayer is thanksgiving for blessings so free,
Prayer is communion, dear Father, with Thee.

30. SWEETNESS EXPOSED

I delight to do thy will.—Psalm 40:8

"I've seen God's lavish beauty across America," says one of God's traveling servants. "But nothing stirs me as does the autumn coloring of the hardwoods. Then I feel like Elizabeth Browning, 'Earth's crammed with heaven, and every common bush afire with God.' In its fall dress the Great Smoky area is my favorite. There gold and russet leaves contrast with dark green evergreens, making each hillside a masterpiece of color."

A leaf is a miracle. It takes sunshine and carbon dioxide from the air, water and nutrients from the soil into its chlorophyll factory. This produces hydrocarbons (sugar), releasing oxygen and water into the air. One oak tree may give off fifty gallons of water on a hot day. Having a tree in one's yard is somewhat like living under an oxygen tent. God marvelously balanced oxygen-inhaling, carbon dioxide-exhaling animals with plants which do the opposite.

With fall comes a killing frost which reveals the sugar in the leaves. Hardship reveals sweetness.

When his wife lay dying with cancer, one staunch Christian testified, "I want to be so filled with the love of God that when I am squeezed, only drops of sweetness come forth." To endure hardship with sweetness of spirit is a true test of Christian character.

> I love thy will, O God,
> The sunshine and the rain,
> Some days are bright with praise,
> Some sweet with accepted pain.

31. LOBO WOLVES

Fear thou not; for I am with thee.—Isaiah
41:10

The lobo farm in western Pennsylvania seemed like
a good place for a rest stop, as the family toured in their
camper. Here in high-fenced pens these fierce wolves
loped restlessly.

The caretaker explained, "Each lobo must have his
separate pen. Lobos are so ravenous that the young must
be taken from the mother at birth. That mother there ate
six of her last litter; but one had survived, hidden behind
the nest. When I found him, he snapped at me so vicious-
ly, I had to put on leather gloves."

Once lobos, timber wolves, roamed much of North
America. They followed the buffalo, attacking the weak
and disabled. Early settlers feared and avoided them.

The Bible warns of three types of spiritual wolves: the
"grievous wolves," false teachers; the persecutors of the
church ,"as sheep among wolves"; and those in the church
who "bite and devour one another."

Christians through the ages have been deceived by false
teachings. Persecution—sometimes violent, sometimes
subtle—has plagued the church. Evil speaking, a wolflike
quality, must be fought personally by each Christian.

But there is one defense: Christ Himself, the Good
Shepherd. He gives whatever is needed to ward off attacks: guidance, courage, or strength.

> I must have the Saviour with me,
> For I dare not walk alone,
> I must feel His presence near me
> And His arms around me thrown.

32. DRIFTWOOD

He is the living God. . . . He delivereth and rescueth.—Daniel 6:26, 27

Gnarled and massive, the stump with branching roots churned in Puget Sound waters. Polished and pruned by sea and sand, it was cast up on the beach during a storm. There it lay until a perceptive person recognized its potential. Now it stands an art form of natural beauty before the Student Union Building at Seattle Pacific College.

Attendants at a "driftwood show" are assured of a fascinating afternoon. Imaginative beachcombers have scoured the shores. They display their finds after transforming them into bits of beauty, comedy, or utility.

Rudy, a son of a judge, once studied for the priesthood. A giant of physical strength, he discovered he liked boxing better than study and became professional. But drink nearly gave him the knockout. In his drifting he wandered into the Olive Branch Mission in Seattle. Later he testified, "That night I got the victory over John Barleycorn and the Man with the Curly Tail [Satan]." God, who knew his potential, transformed his life. Policemen, who once ran him into the drunk tank, gave him a job. He became a trusted officer. Now and then he cooked at camps. Rising early, he made cinnamon rolls for breakfast. Their aroma in baking was the best rising bell ever. He loved to testify to campers how God had rescued and transformed a drifter.

What drifter needs special prayer today for his transformation?

33. CAMPER'S CODE

And the Lord make you to increase and abound in love one toward another.—Hebrews 13:1

At the entrance to the camping area of the state park stood a weathered sign:

CAMPERS' CODE: Leave your camp site just a bit better than you found it.

The family found their assigned spot, backed their trailer into it, and alighted to look around. "Yuk!" exclaimed teen-age Flora. "The last campers here didn't see that sign or else can't read." As Dad helped pick up litter, he moralized: "Remember what I said: there are two kinds of people—mess makers or picker uppers. I'd rather be known for picking up than messing up."

From Cain to today's drug peddlers, history is pocked with names of those who left the world worse than they found it. Just as truly, has the world been blessed by lives of others.

Jake DeShazer hated the Japanese and was glad to be chosen as a Doolittle Raider in World War II. The bombing mission ended in his capture. Imprisoned, he turned to his mother's God. Instead of hatred, God gave him such a love for the Japanese people that following the war, he returned to Japan. For over thirty years he has told the story of God's love to his former enemies. Japan and all the world is better because of Jake's humble but effective life.

Each situation in life offers opportunity for destruction or healing. This day gives opportunity to leave your "camp site" a bit better than you found it.

34. LOVE, NOT WAR

Beloved, let us love one another: for love is of God.—I John 4:7

On the western plains two Indian tribes were encamped side by side as the men joined in a buffalo hunt. One afternoon two boys, one from each tribe, quarreled over a grasshopper. The mothers took up the quarrel, then the fathers. Soon the two tribes were at war. The cause: one grasshopper.

In 1900, Chile and Argentina were preparing for war over their disputed mountain boundary. Bishop Benoventa asked in his Easter sermon, "Why not make friends with our neighbor?" Leaders listened. Before long the two countries signed a Treaty of Arbitration, pledging to arbitrate disputes. To seal their peaceful intents, guns were melted to make the striking statue *Christ of the Andes.* It was placed high on the mountain boundary. At its dedication Chileans and Argentineans knelt at the feet of Christ. They saw His hands outstretched in blessing over them both and realized their brotherhood. Never again have these countries warred.

What causes ill will between persons? Sometimes it seems only grasshopper size; other times, mountainous. If the hurt feelings, animosities, and resentments are taken to the feet of Jesus, love will replace bitterness. As one looks directly into the face of the loving Christ who gave His life for rejecting man, how can hatred remain?

> He drew a circle that shut me out,
> Heretic, rebel, a thing to flout;
> But love and I had the wit to win,
> We drew a circle that took him in.

> —Edwin Markham

35. SOLID ROCK

For thou art my rock and my fortress.—
Psalm 31:3

"Solid Rock Festival," screamed the handbill. A bearded, long-haired youth handed it to high school junior Tim at the street corner. Tim asked, "I dig this rock festival bit, but what's with this *solid* part?"

"Wise up, man," grinned the Jesus Freak. "Jesus Christ, of course, is the Solid Rock. Come hear some real, hard rock music, all about Him! He's neat, man! He's cool!" Then Tim listened to the story of how God had rescued the ex-drug addict from the swampland of sin and set his feet on the Solid Rock, Christ Jesus.

An old man reminisced. "My earliest memories are of awakening in the old farmhouse on the Kansas plains. Mom would be singing as she got breakfast. Times were hard. Crops often failed. One winter we lived mostly on musty cornmeal and jackrabbits. But mother sang on. Her favorite seemed to be, 'On Christ, the Solid Rock, I stand; all other ground is sinking sand.' "

The psalmists of Israel lived in a land of many rock outcroppings. They loved their rocky land. Its towering rocks served as fortresses from their enemies. No wonder the psalms are full of references to God as a rock.

Whether it be for the ancient Israelite, the pioneer, or today's needy one, God and His Son Christ Jesus offer solidity, strength, and security in an unstable world.

> His oath, his covenant, his blood
> Support me in the whelming flood;
> When all around my soul gives way,
> He then is all my hope and stay.

36. FOSSILS

Draw nigh to God, and he will draw nigh to you.—James 4:8

A popular craft at camps is embedding nature specimens in resin—liquid plastic which quickly hardens. Recently along the Baltic coast of Germany, a fossil hunter found a fly embedded in resin. Hardly unusual—except that experts declared the resin to be hardened amber—and it and the fly twenty million years old!

Fossils are records of living things preserved in the earth's crust. These may be the items themselves, as bones or teeth; or stone casts, like footprints; or prints of ferns or leaves in stone; or the most common fossil, petrified matter.

Petrifaction occurs when living cells of wood are gradually replaced with minerals which harden into stone.

Irreverent young people were known to add to the testimony of one in their church in whom they did not have full confidence: "I'm saved, sanctified — *and petrified!*"

Too often those who have been lively Christians gradually lose that vitality that once characterized their Christian lives. Christian duty becomes habit without joy. Christian patterns of life become routine. But gone is the glow of life, the sparkle in the testimony, and the urge to witness. The cure: a fresh anointing of the power and joy of the Holy Spirit. How willing God is to give this! For every small step of man's "drawing nigh," God takes a giant step to meet him.

37. STRENGTH FOR DISASTER

*I can do all things in Christ, which strength-
eneth me.*—I Thessalonians 4:13

Floods, tragedy, disaster! Few lives are spared some
form of terrifyingly real, soul-shattering disaster: finan-
cial collapse, ill health, disappointment with loved ones, or
death of those nearest and dearest. And in spite of tech-
nological marvels which pamper modern man, he still
stands helpless in the face of natural, physical disaster.

Hurricane Agnes brought ravaging floods in June 1972.
Pennsylvania's governor labeled it "the greatest disaster
ever to hit our nation." Statisticians tallied: "dead, 118;
homeless, 400,000; homes and businesses destroyed,
100,000; property damage, three billion dollars." But
statistics cannot measure the terror of escape, the grief
for lost loved ones, or the pain of going back to water-
logged or vanished property. One survivor reported: "I
found my yard, but there was no house. On my lot were
three roofs, none of them mine."

An editor commented, "Perhaps the most discourag-
ing part of the disaster is the moment of mopping up
the mess. Even then despair quickly is overtaken by
the desire to rebuild, reclaim, and in many instances
start anew."

The Christian facing the task of "mopping up" after
personal disaster is sustained by God's promises. The
apostle Paul faced one crisis after another. In words that
have echoed down the centuries, he reveals his unfail-
ing resource: "Christ which strengtheneth me."

38. ANTS ON THE SIDEWALK

Go to the ant, thou sluggard, consider her ways, and be wise.—Proverbs 6:6

Prison chaplain Carl Burke explained God to a troubled ghetto youth, "God is like a father." "Ha," spat out the youth, "if he's like mine, I would sure hate him." Burke found the Bible a closed book to these youth who had no concept of love. Later they assisted him in translating Scripture portions into their own idiom, making it meaningful to them.

Ants, the most intelligent of insects, have a message for such youth, as much as for the sluggards of Solomon's time:

Take a look at the ants on the sidewalk.
Think about how they work and you'll be with it, man;
They don't got a worker to checkup on them—right!
They get their own food then put it away till they need it.
Don't need no government surplus stuff.
So don't be a lazy bum and sleep all day—
Get up and go shine shoes.
Sleep's a good thing at night, but too much is too much—
And a lazy cat ends up on welfare. It just sneaks up on you.
A lazy guy is like a hood. You can't believe anything he says.
He's got shifty pincers,
Always blaming someone for his troubles
Always trying to con a guy and stir up trouble.[1]

What does such street language have to do with Christians who can afford to go camping? Two things: stir them to action and prayer for such youth; inspire them to make Scripture relevant to their own lives.

---

[1] Carl F. Burke, *God Is for Real, Man* (New York: Association Press, 1966). Used by permission.

39. SHUT-OFF SWITCH

Study to be quiet.—I Thessalonians 4:11

Except for its seventy boy campers, the primitive camp site was a haven of quiet and serenity. Only a small area had been cleared by its private lake front for essential buildings. The rest of the beautiful Pennsylvania forest-land remained as it had been for hundreds of years.

It was bedtime, the first night of camp. Boys were bedded down in clusters of tents. Their thin walls did little to stop conversation bouncing from tent to tent. Counselors did their best to quiet the overstimulated boys. Finally one counselor, tired himself and completely frustrated, asked the camp director, "How do you find the shut-off switch for these motor mouths?"

Sometimes quieting one's heart before God seems as difficult as trying to quiet the mouths of seventy excited campers. Even away from routine when camping, one can become so caught up in activities that a quiet time is neglected. Yet finding a place to be alone and quiet with God is essential.

> Drop thy still dews of quietness,
> Till all our strivings cease;
> Take from our souls the strain and stress,
> And let our ordered lives confess
> The beauty of thy peace.
>   —John G. Whittier

40. CAUGHT UP?

Blessed be the Lord, who daily loadeth us with benefits.—Psalm 68:19

Edward Bok emigrated from Helder, Netherlands, to Brooklyn at the age of six. His was the typical "rags to riches" story in America, the land of opportunity. He became editor of leading magazines, writer of best sellers. Grateful for his opportunities here, he wanted to express his appreciation by a gift to the American people.

On Florida's highest hill he purchased land for the Mountain Lake Bird Sanctuary. Here, near Lake Wales, he erected the famous "Singing Tower." Its architectural beauty is matched only by the concerts from its seventy-one bell carillon. Nightingales and mockingbirds in the sanctuary vie with the bells in ethereal harmony. The thousands of tourists who visit the shrine are blessed by Edward Bok's gift of beauty—his expression of love for America.

Few can give as generously as did Edward Bok. But each citizen can build a shrine of gratitude in his own heart for the blessings he enjoys in his nation.

Jesus, having healed ten lepers, was thanked by only one. He questioned, "Where are the nine?"

If one spends a few moments reflecting on God's myriad benefits, can he feel that he is "caught up" on praise due to God?

41. SEQUOIA GIGANTEA

*Well done, thou good and faithful servant . . .
enter thou into the joy of thy lord.*—Matthew 25:21

"Unbelievable!" The Fremont exploration party were awe-struck. Descending the Sierras into California, they had stumbled onto a forest of giant trees, some rising more than three hundred feet. Huge trunks towered seventy-five feet before the first branch stretched outward. Their evergreen needles were flat like juniper, and their cones as small as robins' eggs. "They must have been here when Christ walked the earth," one explorer guessed correctly.

"What shall we name them?" asked General Fremont. Looking at their Indian interpreter, one suggested, "Let's call them Sequoia." Since then these oldest and largest of living things have been called *Sequoia gigantea*.

Born in the brave but fierce Cherokee tribe, Sequoia was converted in the Brainerd Mission on Missionary Ridge in Tennessee. In adult life, he was honored as inventor of the Cherokee alphabet. When General Fremont came seeking an interpreter for his expedition to chart the West, Sequoia was a teen-ager. Missionaries were reluctant to let their brilliant Christian lad go with the rough explorers. "I believe he can do it and keep true to Christ," said one.

Each morning in camp Sequoia sought a place of prayer to ask God to keep him true. His ungodly companions showed their respect by naming these noble trees for the boy. His life pattern was that of a spiritual giant.

Daily devotions still enable one to stand straight and tall, no matter what the day may bring.

42. TALL TOPS

Trust in the living God who giveth us all things richly to enjoy.—I Timothy 6:17

"TREES OF MYSTERY." Nearly every car the Scotts met on the Redwood highway flaunted this fluorescent bumper sticker. "Let's stop there, dad," pleaded Bob. "Probably just another tourist trap," dad judged; "but, okay, we'll stop."

Even Bob's exuberance subsided as he hiked the trail between the giant redwoods. Soon the family stood reverently before the Cathedral tree, a semicircle of stately redwoods, and read the rustic sign:

> This is their temple vaulted high,
> And here we pause with reverent eye,
> With silent tongue and awe-struck soul;
> For here we see life's proper goal.
> To be like these, straight, true and fine,
> To make our world, like theirs, a shrine,
> Sink down, O traveler, on your knees,
> God stands before you in these trees.

These masterpieces of God's handiwork are found in seventy-five thousand acres of public parkland. The redwoods, *Sequoia sempervirens,* are cousins of the *Sequoia gigantea* of the Sierras. The redwoods are taller, growing only in the coastal strip, where their tops are bathed in Pacific fog and mist. Their lacy needles are like hemlock and tiny cones as small as wrens' eggs.

Whether or not one has visited a redwood forest, each can rejoice in the creator, who so richly gives us things of joy.

43. POTTER AND CLAY

But now, O Lord, thou art our father; we are the clay and thou our potter.—Isaiah 64:8

Planning crafts for camp, the camp director visited a ceramic factory. He was delighted to find the owner to be a Christian. As he conducted a tour of his plant, the owner wove in his testimony.

"From this cliff behind the plant we dig the clay, separating it for a life of usefulness. I remember when Christ dug me from my sinful life, and I left the world behind.

"In this cleaning room, we wash and screen the clay, removing impurities. Thank God for the day He washed me in the blood of Christ and forgave my sins.

"Here oil is added to make the clay easier to work. Oil is a symbol of the Holy Spirit. The indwelling Spirit of Christ fills the Christian with love for others.

"The clay really takes punishment here, pounded to remove air, pressed in heavy molds, fired in heated kilns. But all the time, the potter is watching. Troubles? Trials? I've had them, but God has always been near.

"In this storage room vessels await orders. Not one is exactly like another. But all are useful and are sent all over the country to serve. God knows best where to place His people."

Have thine own way, Lord,
Have thine own way.
Thou art the potter, I am the clay;
Mold me and make me after thy will,
While I am waiting, yielded and still.

44. BUILDING FOR LIFE

*Except the Lord build the house, they labour
in vain that build it.*—Psalm 127:1

Sanibel Island, shell hunter's paradise, hangs like a
jewel on Florida's Gulf Coast. One sunny morning on its
beach, a family delighted in hunting miniature shells.
As father drew in the net from the rolling surf, excited
children clustered around. "There's a bloody tooth, an
ivory tusk, a murex!" they shouted.

Incredibly built by soft mollusks, shells have long fascinated man. For centuries they have been used in art
and jewelry, or as money. Shells vary from those of the
tiny scavenger snails in the fish bowl to the mammoth
ones of the South Seas.

Oliver Wendell Holmes immortalized the small mollusk
which builds each season a new room in its lustrous,
spiral shell. "The Chambered Nautilus" draws a pointed
lesson for man:

Year after year beheld the silent toil
That spread his lustrous coil;
Still, as the spiral grew,
He left the past year's dwelling for the new,
Stole with soft step its shining archway through,
Built up its idle door,
Stretched in his last-found home, and knew the old no
more.

Build thee more stately mansions, O my soul,
As the swift seasons roll!
Leave thy low-vaulted past!
Let each new temple, nobler than the last,
Shut thee from heaven with a dome more vast,
Till thou at length art free,
Leaving thine outgrown shell by life's unresting sea!

45. SAND CASTLES

If any man's work abide which he hath built thereupon, he shall receive a reward.—I Corinthians 3:14

Fortunate is the camp which lies just over the sand dunes from the Pacific Ocean. Naturally the camp program is sea-oriented. Surf-jumping, fishing, beachcombing are favorite recreations. Crafts are shell- and driftwood-dominated.

One afternoon teen-agers cooperated to build what had to be one of the most intricate sand castles ever. "Fantastic!" they agreed as they took a last look before disappearing over the sand dunes as the supper bell rang.

But during the night the rising tide leveled the fabulous structure. In the morning there was only smooth, wet sand.

In Cannon Beach, Oregon, each year a sand castle competition is staged. Prizes reward the most imaginative builders. But their efforts, too, are leveled by relentless tides.

Sand is great for building sand castles. But in building a life, one wants sturdier materials. The apostle Paul in allegory suggests that gold, silver, and precious stones are suitable materials for life-building; wood, hay, and stubble are unsuitable.

Each Christian may well examine his life structure. What will endure when death's relentless tide comes flooding in?

46. MOUNTAIN TOP

We were witnesses of his majesty . . . when we were with him in the holy mount.—II Peter 1:16, 18

To climb the rugged slopes of snow-capped Mount Jefferson in Oregon's mid-Cascades seemed an impossible dream. But Scoutmaster White encouraged his young scouts, "You can do it. I'll go with you." After weeks of planning and a hard climb, the patrol reached the summit. For Eagle Scout Elton Higbee, it was a high moment. Triumphantly he signed his name in the summit register.

Another high moment for Elton came while he was a freshman in a Christian college. "I have given my life to Christ," he wrote his minister parents.

Life took Elton to Guam for service in World War II, and to a stint in the business world. But he felt the call back to the mountains and valleys of Oregon. He worked happily on his peppermint farm, nestled near the foothills of the Cascades. Often as he piloted his mechanized equipment across the fields, he looked to the mountains, remembering his two high moments. His trip to Jefferson's summit gave him confidence in himself; his conversion gave him confidence that God guided his life.

God had another high moment for Elton. On Mother's Day after church he drove with his family to take his mother a gift. A curve, a careening truck in the wrong lane, a head-on crash! Instantly Elton was with his Savior. Now his body lies in a hillside cemetery, facing the mountains that inspired him in life.

The apostle Peter treasured the memory of his moments on the Mount of Transfiguration long years afterward. For every Christian, spiritual mountain-top experiences give inspiration and encouragement.

47. EXPLOITS

*The people that do know their God shall be
strong and do exploits.*—Daniel 11:32

Have you seen any spider webs lately? Consider them
as one of God's marvels. The spider is not the usual six-
legged, three-body-part insect. It is an arachnid: an eight-
legged, two-body-part creature, a relative of the crab. As
a master engineer it spins, then positions its anchor strands
for a sure foundation. Then it constructs the center spiral
of its web from sticky filaments to attract its prey.

One naturalist carefully sprays spider webs with white
paint. He then detaches them and mounts their fragile
beauty on dark paper to decorate the walls of his study.

Robert Bruce, Scotland's king of the fourteenth century, had been defeated on the battlefield. Alone, hiding
from enemies in a cave, he was discouraged with his fight
to free his people. In the bright sunlight of the cave entrance, he observed a spider attempting to anchor its web.
Time and again it was thwarted as the wind carried its
strands awry. Undaunted, the spider kept at it. Finally
the completed web shimmered in the sunlight. Encouraged, Bruce resolved, "If the spider can try until it suc-
ceeds, I will, too." He left the cave to rally his forces and
liberate Scotland.

Eliza Cook, poet of the last century, wrote:

> Whenever you find your heart despairs
> Of doing some good thing,
> Con over this strain, try bravely again
> And remember the Spider and King.

The same God, who gives skill and courage to His small
creatures, will enable His people to succeed in the tasks
He assigns.

48. FORK IN THE TRAIL

And the Lord shall guide thee continually.
—Isaiah 58:11

The camp director was worried. It was suppertime. One cabin group was still not back from the afternoon hike through the wilderness area adjoining the camp site. But as the director planned a search party, a string of boys and their counselor emerged from the wooded trail. Freckled-faced Denny still had energy to sprint toward the director. "We took the wrong fork in the trail!" he shouted.

In the pine forests of eastern Washington, Harold was a first-time camper. "I was at the fork of the trail," he remembers. "From an unchurched home, I was becoming involved with an ungodly crowd. A pastor friend persuaded me to go to camp. There I made the decision to go Christ's way. That camp was the turning point in my life and the reason I am a pastor now myself."

Every attendant at a Christian camp stands at the fork of a trail. He will leave camp traveling with firmer step along the trail of life with Christ. Or he will leave inwardly sorrowing, like the rich young ruler, because he chose the path leaving Christ behind.

Whether at camp or not, is not every day, every decision a forked trail? But God promises guidance!

49. WILLING WORKERS

Thy will be done in earth, as it is in heaven.
—Matthew 6:10

Near Fort Wayne, Indiana, an inspired camp director sided a beehive with glass. He placed the hive just inside the nature house, making an entrance for the bees through the back wall. Fascinated campers safely watched the bees at work.

Bees work in unbelievable cooperation. The male drones are nonworkers. The fertilized queen lays up to fifteen hundred eggs a day and may work as long as three years. Female workers may number as many as fifty thousand in one hive. Hive workers feed the larvae and control temperature and humidity by fanning. Nectar, converted by secreted enzymes and evaporation, is stored as honey. Foraging bees fly as far as several miles for nectar, pollen, or water. Guards and scouts know their duties. With an incredible wig-wag of their abdomen, returning bees indicate in a dance the source of nectar. All are motivated to keep the hive prosperous, well fed, clean, and warm. Instinctively each bee senses what needs to be done, changing tasks as needed. Who knows what inner voice directs them?

The complicated task of building God's kingdom requires unbelievable cooperation. Who can count the tasks to be done or the talents needed? But as each of His children obey God's voice, God's will is accomplished. How essential it is to listen and obey!

Only one life, 'twill soon be past,
Only what's done for Christ will last.

50. DUCK CALL

The steps of a good man are ordered by the Lord.—Psalm 37:23

"Ducks in the street again," guessed the driver as traffic backed up on Park Avenue. Winona Lake, Indiana, advertises itself as "Home of the World's Largest Bible Conference." Summer conference attendants throng the village to hear America's great speakers in the Billy Sunday Tabernacle. Ducks, too, are summer residents. Half-tame from much attention, they waddle across the road to the lake, unconcerned about traffic jams.

By fall, conference attendants have gone home. Like all waterfowl, Winona's ducks begin to hear the call to winter feeding grounds.

His observation of waterfowl gave William Cullen Bryant inspiration for a timeless message. His poem "To a Waterfowl" is acclaimed as "America's greatest short poem."

> Whither, 'midst falling dew,
> While glow the heavens with the last steps of day,
> Far, through their rosy depths, dost thou pursue
> Thy solitary way? . . .
>
> There is a Power whose care
> Teaches thy way along that pathless coast—
> The desert and illimitable air—
> Lone wandering, but not lost. . . .
>
> Thou'rt gone! the abyss of heaven
> Hath swallowed up thy form; yet, on my heart
> Deeply has sunk the lesson thou hast given,
> And shall not soon depart.
>
> He, who, from zone to zone
> Guides through the boundless sky thy certain flight,
> In the long way that I must tread alone,
> Will lead my steps aright.

51. BIGFOOT

The fool hath said in his heart, There is no God.—Psalm 14:1

Sasquatch, Bigfoot, the Abominable Snowman—is he, or isn't he? This has been debated for over a hundred years from California to the Yukon. Indian legends tell of their people's fear of this creature: giant, hairy, bad-smelling, manlike. From the days of the Hudson Bay trappers and California gold miners, sightings, tracks, mysterious killings, nests, and other evidences have been reported.

Now Roger Patterson has movie films of an apelike creature he reportedly photographed in northern California. Experts calculate this "Bigfoot" to be seven feet tall, weighing 350 pounds. These pictures only add to the debate: "A hoax, a man in an ape suit!" But one confirmed unbeliever comments, "Won't we be surprised if searchers come down the mountain leading one by the hand?"

Is there a God or isn't there? "Only a man-made invention," says the unbeliever. "Only the fool does not believe in God," replies the Bible lover.

Stock market analyst Richard Russel recently wrote: "In my younger and more ignorant days, I fancied myself an atheist, then an agnostic. . . . I have become convinced beyond a shadow of a doubt that there is a supreme and infinite intelligence that guides the life of man and the universe."

Tourists once asked a leading scientist in the Mount Palomar Observatory, "Do you believe in God?" The reply: "As a scientist, I can do nothing else but believe that an intelligent God planned and rules the universe."

How doubts fade when one meets the living Christ!

52. TREASURES AT HOME

In the house of the righteous is much treasure.
—Proverbs 15:6

In India, the legend goes, a prosperous farmer was visited by a passing priest. The priest spun an exciting tale about diamond hunting. Impressed, the farmer sold his farm to a neighbor and began a quest for diamonds. Traveling far, spending his means, losing his health, he died far from home, never finding a diamond.

One day the priest again visited the farm. On the mantel he noticed a rock. "Oh, I see the former owner has returned with his diamond." "No, that's just a rock I picked up here," said the new owner. "I know a diamond when I see one," replied the priest. It was a diamond. The treasure for which the former owner had wasted his means and life could have been found right at home.

What treasures in one's own home lie undiscovered, unused, or only half-appreciated?

Both parents and young people may with profit examine their home lives. Are the precious treasures of love from parents, children, or siblings appreciated sufficiently? Are opportunities being seized to show Christian attitudes? Is the jewel of gratitude evident often enough? What rich treasures may be discovered right at home as family members join in the search!

53. STORMS AND PINPRICKS

My grace is sufficient for thee.—II Corinthians 12:9

Myron crouched under the low branches of a huge maple on the wooded Midwest camp site. The storm had struck suddenly. Crash! A towering red oak smashed across the tent from which Myron's sister had fled moments before. A giant maple banged onto a nearby cabin. Myron ducked as a branch swished by his head. Torrential rains drenched him. Then suddenly the storm ended. Myron and other campers crept out to view the devastated camp. There had been no loss of life! A broken arm was the only injury.

Storms are an inevitable part of weather. The weather bureau classifies them as local showers, general rain, scattered thundershowers, tornadoes, and hurricanes. The bureau can classify and predict, but it has done little to modify storms.

Storms are just as inevitable and unpredictable in personal lives as they are in nature. They vary from the light local showers of everyday annoyances to the "sudden storms that leave us stunned and breathless." God, who predicted the coming of storms to every Christian, also promises a sufficiency of grace for every need.

His grace is great enough to meet the great things—
  The crashing waves that overwhelm the soul,
The roaring winds that leave us stunned and breathless,
  The sudden storms beyond our life's control.

His grace is great enough to meet the small things—
  The little pin-prick troubles that annoy,
The insect worries, buzzing and persistent,
  The squeaking wheels that grate upon our joy.[1]
                          —Annie Johnson Flint

[1] By permission of Evangelical Publishers, Toronto, Canada.

54. NURSE LOGS

He being dead yet speaketh.—Hebrews 11:4

Charles, the camp naturalist, took his campers into the primitive area of the camp. They clambered in the coolness of the shaded forest over fallen branches and logs, among the fern and brambles.

Pointing to a moss-covered, fallen giant, now reuniting with the soil, Charles said, "This tree may have fallen a hundred years ago. It is called a nurse log. Can you guess why?" Campers quickly realized the reason for the name. Younger trees rose in a straight row along the top of the old log. As seedlings they had sprouted in its damp moss and now continued to grow, drawing nutrients from their nurse log.

Back in the cleared area of the camp, Charles pointed out, "Notice these clumps of mature trees? The nurse logs are long gone. But to those who understand such things, it is evident where they once were."

Older Christians are often discouraged when life lays them low. Unable to be as active as formerly, they question their usefulness. But only God knows how the stored-up richness and sweetness of their lives is still helping others.

Young people often are so unaware of the help they are receiving from older Christians. Even those long dead have inspired those close at hand who now minister to the young.

All are debtors to the past and donors to the future.

55. ONE GENERATION TO ANOTHER

One generation shall praise thy works to another.—Psalm 145:4

Pious Turnidges crossed the continent in the first waves of settlers westward. From the British Isles they came to North Carolina in the early 1700s. Onward they went following Daniel Boone through Kentucky, Tennessee, and later to Missouri.

As a baby, John Turnidge rode one of the first Union Pacific emigrant trains westward from Missouri. His father, Joseph Elijah, civil war veteran, settled in the Oregon foothills, carving a homestead from the dense Douglas fir forests. When John married, his father gave him land on which to build a cabin for his bride. Both products of centuries of pious living, John and Alice made Bible precepts the rule of life in their home. Children (and grandchildren) have vivid memories of family prayer time before breakfast, all taking turns reading God's Word. Kindly "Brother John," farmer, freight hauler with wagon and team, was also an unordained elder. His neighbors showed their respect by asking him 150 times to preach the simple funerals of their loved ones.

In retirement he moved to a modern home in a small town. There he became known as "Lebanon's Walking Bible." At ninety years of age he was welcomed as he made his rounds to hospitals and rest homes. He could quote from memory most passages of the New Testament and many from the Old. When he died in 1961, over one hundred descendants thanked God for the influence of his life.

Question: When will John's influence—and your influence—end?

56. PRAYER PATH

Pray without ceasing. In everything give thanks.—I Thessalonians 5:17

"Jossefa, something is wrong with your prayer path!" reproved Simoni, the African national pastor. Jossefa was a new convert in the village. He had been instructed to find a prayer spot in the bush and use it regularly for his quiet time with God. Regular use would keep the weeds in the pathway tramped down. But Jossefa's pastor had noticed the path was becoming overgrown, evidence that Jossefa's prayer life was neglected.

A famous pianist reported, "I practice regularly five hours a day. If I neglect one day, I notice it; two days, my musician friends notice it; three days, my audience notices it."

Probably God is the first to know when His child forgets to fellowship with Him. Then the Christian becomes aware of a leanness in his soul. Before long, if prayer is neglected, others will know that the Christian has been neglecting "his prayer path."

Lord, what a change with us one short hour
Spent in Thy presence will prevail to make!
. . . Why, therefore, should we do ourselves this wrong,
Or others that we are not always strong,
That we are ever overborne with care,
That we should ever weak or heartless be,
Anxious or troubled, when with us in prayer,
And joy and strength and courage are with Thee.
—Archbishop Trench

57. CEDARS OF LEBANON

The desert shall rejoice . . . the glory of Lebanon shall be given unto it.—Isaiah 35:1, 2

Nearly every reference to Lebanon in the Bible speaks of the beauty of this land which borders Palestine. Ancient Lebanon was famed for its mountain slopes forested with cedars. These *cedrus libani* held the moisture of the melting snows from off the mountains, protecting fertility of the valleys below.

King Solomon began to build the temple at Jerusalem about 1000 B.C. He obtained Lebanon cedars from King Hiram. "Four thousand hewers in the mountains" cut timbers for the temple, seven years in building. This was just one instance in the devastation of Lebanon's forests.

After centuries of human exploitation, the slopes of Lebanon are now eroded. The famed cedars are reduced to about four hundred trees, enclosed by a rocky fence. The rich soil has been washed away; much of the rocky land is useful only for goats.

But there is hope. Reforestation has begun. Perhaps the mountains of Lebanon will regain their glory, and the desert again rejoice.

God's natural law is that tree-carpeted hillsides retain moisture and soil; barren hillsides will erode and cause floods.

God has other laws—spiritual laws of human conduct. Men may break God's laws for their own immediate pleasure, but this does not change the law. Man inevitably suffers the consequences.

But there is hope—for Lebanon's mountains and for the repentant sinner.

58. THY WILL BE DONE

After this manner, pray ye. . . . Thy will be done on earth as it is in heaven.—Matthew 6:9, 10

Anyone who has tried raising a vegetable garden will identify with Karel Capek in his "Gardener's Prayer."

"O Lord, grant that in some way it may rain every day, say from about midnight until three o'clock in the morning . . . gentle and warm so that it can soak in . . . that there may be plenty of dew and little wind, enough worms, no plant-lice, and snails, no mildew, and that once a week thin liquid manure and guano may fall from heaven."

Another prayer which may get as far with the Lord as author Capek's is this old farmer's: "Lord bless my son John and his wife, me and my wife, us four, no more. Amen."

In northern India tribesmen write out their prayers, insert the paper in rattle-shaped prayer wheels, and give them a whirl now and then.

The Christian, when he prays, will not pray either selfishly or routinely. Christ demonstrated this in the Garden of Gethsemane: "Nevertheless, not my will but thine be done." Seeking God's will over one's own is an essential of true prayer.

> Teach me to pray, Lord, teach me to pray,
> This is my heart cry, day unto day,
> I long to know thy will and thy way;
> Teach me to pray, Lord, teach me to pray.

59. GRINDSTONES AND BEAUTY

I know thy works and thy labour.—Revelation 2:2

Wordsworth noted:

> The world is too much with us,
> Late and soon, getting and spending,
> We lay waste our powers. . . .

A more modern unknown poet advises:

If you put your nose to the grindstone rough
And keep it down there long enough,
You'll soon forget there are such things
As brooks that babble and birds that sing,
Three things shall all your world compose:
Just you, the grindstone, and—your poor old nose!

All of this leads one to want to shuck off the workaday routine, to strike off into the hills with a shiny new camper, trailer, motor home (for the affluent), or backpack (for the athletic). "Brooks that babble and birds that sing" do give surcease to routine-caused wounds of the spirit. Thank God for vacation days!

But there is a glory, too, "a high stern-featured beauty of plain devotedness to duty." James Russell Lowell gives a lift of spirits to those who must return to the task:

> The longer on this earth we live
> And weigh the various qualities of men
> The more we feel the high stern-featured beauty
> Of plain devotedness to duty,
> Steadfast and still, nor paid with mortal praise,
> But finding amplest recompense
> For life's ungarlanded expense
> In work done squarely and unwasted days.

Thank God, too, for the privilege of work!

60. SLOW ME DOWN, LORD

Open my eyes that I may see wondrous things.
—Psalm 119:18

Campers on the path to the lake had more on their mind this morning than seeing who would be first off the swimming dock. Clustered about the camp naturalist, they were fascinated as he opened their eyes to God's marvels all about them.

"Wow," said Ronald, "I've hiked this trail a dozen times and have never seen all this stuff. I guess I went too fast!"

Orin L. Crain has some wise words for all of us:

"Slow me down, Lord! Ease the pounding of my heart by the quieting of my mind. Steady my hurried pace with a vision of the eternal reach of time. Give me, amidst the confusion of my day, the calmness of the everlasting hills. Break the tension of my nerves with the soothing music of the singing streams that live in my memory.

"Help me to know the magical restoring power of sleep. Teach me the art of taking minute vacations, of slowing down to look at a flower; to chat with an old friend or make a new one; to pat a stray dog; to watch a spider build a web; to smile at a child; or to read a few lines from a good book. Remind me each day that the race is not always to the swift; that there is more to life than increasing its speed.

"Let me look upward into the branches of the towering oak and know that it grew great and strong because it grew slowly and well.

"Slow me down, Lord, and inspire me to send my roots deep into the soil of life's enduring values, that I may grow toward the stars of my greater destiny."